How do you like our book?

We would really appreciate you leaving us a review.

Other Picture Books:

For other fun Picture Books by Kampelstone,
simply search for:

Kampelstone Picture Books

D1710045

Facts about Flamingos

- Adult flamingos are four to five ft (1.2-1.5 m) tall and their wingspans range from 3.3 to 5 ft (1-1.5 m) wide. Even so, they only weigh from 4-8 lb (1.8-3.2 kg)

- Flamingo feathers are naturally gray. The pink color of flamingo feathers results from pigments called carotenoids which occur naturally in the brine-shrimp and blue-green algae that they eat. The more of the pigment they consume, the stronger the color of pink in their feathers.

- Flamingos often stand on one leg. It's not known why, but some scientists believe that flamingos can save more energy standing on one leg than on two. Another theory is that they do this to conserve body heat in the cold water of their feeding areas. Because their legs can lock into position, it requires no effort to stand and they can even sleep in this position swaying in the wind but not falling over.

- Before taking off in flight, flamingos need to run to build up speed. Even when they're in water they can run since they have webbing between their toes.

- A group of flamingos is called either a flamboyance. Other words sometimes used to describe a group of flamingos are a regiment, a stand or a colony. Flamingos are very social and a flamboyance of flamingos can number well into the thousands.

- Both the male and the female feed their chicks with crop milk which is a secretion from the esophagus of the birds that is high in fats and proteins.

- There are six distinct species of flamingo: greater flamingo, lesser flamingo, James's flamingo, Chilean flamingo, Andean flamingo, and American flamingo.

- Flamingos tend to congregate in mudflats or lagoons, where they can find shallow saltwater prey. These habitats are also difficult for predators to negotiate.

- Flamingos feed by first stirring up the mud with their feet. Then, with their head in an upside down position, they scoop up a beakful of mud and water. Flamingos don't have teeth but their beaks and tongues are lined with lamellae, hair-like structures that filter out the silt from their food.

- The American flamingo is the only flamingo species native to North America. It is generally more brightly colored than the Greater flamingo.

- The Greater flamingo is the most widespread species; it inhabits the coasts of Africa, Asia, and southern Europe. The most numerous is the Lesser flamingo.

- The people of Ancient Rome were known to eat flamingo tongues as a delicacy.

- Flamingos can fly up to 10,000-15,000 feet.

- Flamingos fly at a speed of 30-37 mph (50-60 kph) and cover a distance up to 370 miles (600 km).

- Flamingo eggs are similar to chickenNEggs: white on the outside and yellow on the inside though sometimes the yolk can be pink.

- Baby flamingos aren't born with curved beaks.

Made in United States
Orlando, FL
03 April 2022